BOLIVIA 2016 HUMAN RIGHTS REPORT

Note: This report was updated 4/13/17; see Appendix F: Errata for more information.

EXECUTIVE SUMMARY

Bolivia is a constitutional, multiparty republic with an elected president and a bicameral legislature. In October 2014, in a process deemed free but whose fairness was questioned by international observers, citizens re-elected President Evo Morales Ayma, leader of the Movement Toward Socialism Party (MAS), for a third term. On February 21, the government held a referendum to allow the president a fourth term in office. Citizens voted the measure down in a process that international observers deemed mostly fair and free.

Civilian authorities maintained effective control over the security forces.

The most serious human rights problems included severe restrictions on freedom of press and association and the use of the judiciary to limit independent media outlets and political opposition. Widespread corruption and inefficiency in the country's law enforcement and judicial system, leading to denial of a fair and timely public trial, and harsh prison conditions were also rampant.

Additional human rights problems included abuse by police and military officials, lack of government transparency, violence against women, trafficking in persons, vigilante justice, poor labor conditions, and child labor. Despite recent legislative advances, societal discrimination continued against lesbian, gay, bisexual, and transgender, and intersex (LGBTI) persons. Discrimination affected other vulnerable groups, including women, members of racial and ethnic minority groups, individuals with disabilities, indigenous persons, and those with HIV/AIDS.

Although the government took steps in some cases to prosecute security service and other government officials who committed abuses, inconsistent application of the law and a dysfunctional judiciary led to impunity.

Section 1. Respect for the Integrity of the Person, Including Freedom from:

a. Arbitrary Deprivation of Life and other Unlawful or Politically Motivated Killings

Several news outlets reported that national police officers committed unlawful killings in the shooting deaths of three miners during the course of August protests between the National Federation of Mining Cooperatives and police. The government's decision to amend the Cooperatives Law to allow the unionization of subcontractors within the cooperative sparked the protests, which lasted from August 10 to August 26. Fermin Mamani, Severi Ichota, and Ruben Aparaya died of gunshot wounds during the protests, despite government claims that police used nonlethal bullets to quell the demonstrations. The Vice Minister of Interior, Rodolfo Illanes, was negotiating with the miners on behalf of the government when protesters captured, tortured, and eventually killed him. Authorities arrested 11 protest leaders in connection with the death of the vice minister. On October 6, the Ombudsman's Office publicly stated that, under the authority of Minister of Government Carlos Romero, police used lethal ammunition against the miners. On October 27, Human Rights Ombudsman David Tezanos presented his office's official findings to the State Prosecutor. Their investigations stated that "at least seven" police personnel used lethal firearms in the miner's conflict. Two of the miners who were publicly implicated in the killing of Illanes called the findings of the Ombudsman's office false.

b. Disappearance

There were no reports of politically motivated disappearances.

c. Torture and Other Cruel, Inhuman, or Degrading Treatment or Punishment

The constitution prohibits all forms of torture, coercion, and physical and emotional violence. Despite these regulations there were credible reports that government officials employed them. Although no laws specifically prohibit torture, it is more generally covered under penal code provisions on respecting the right to physical integrity. The penal code carries only minimum penalties for those found guilty; no public official has ever been found guilty under those provisions.

On August 17, police officers guarding prisoners in the Pando prison reportedly tortured multiple detainees in an attempt to gather information about an investigation underway at the time. As of October there was no official number of victims. Police reportedly beat the prisoners and subjected them to electric shocks and tear-gassing, and men, women, and children were all among the alleged victims of police violence. The Ministry of Justice and the Prosecutor's Office were investigating the case. The Institute of Therapy and Investigation (ITEI), a credible nongovernmental organization (NGO), was also conducting an independent investigation.

ITEI stated that the most frequent perpetrators of torture and mistreatment were members of the Bolivian National Police and military officials. ITEI reports indicated that police relied heavily on torture as the first form of investigation to procure information and extract confessions. The majority of these abuses reportedly occurred while officials were transferring detainees to police facilities or while the prisoners were held in detention. According to credible reports from NGO employees who worked with prison populations, the most common forms of torture for detainees included the use of Tasers, asphyxiation, verbal abuse, and verbal threats of violence.

Within the military torture and mistreatment reportedly occurred both to punish and to intimidate trainees into submission and obedience. Reports indicated that military officials regularly verbally abused soldiers for minor infractions and perceived disobedience. In January a regimental commander was recorded on video verbally abusing a sergeant under his command for questioning one of the commander's orders. The National Council of the Defense of the Constitution brought charges of discrimination (a criminal offense) against the commander for his actions. According to sources this type of verbal abuse and hazing in the armed forces was not uncommon. In January then human rights ombudsman Rolando Villena reported that at least 30 soldiers died in military service in the last three years.

On April 23, the then human rights ombudsman, Rolando Villena, reported his office received and processed 19,097 cases of "violations of human rights" in 2015, a 647 percent increase from 2014. Of the cases his office examined during 2015, the following violations occurred with the most frequency: 17 percent involved the right to due process and access to justice, 13 percent involved workers' rights, 12 percent involved property and personal property, 8 percent involved the right to petition, and 7 percent involved a lack of accessibility for individuals wishing to obtain personal identification documents. Villena stated that officials working under the judiciary and police forces perpetrated the most abuses. The ombudsman also stated that despite the trend of rising violations against human rights, the legislature had never accepted his suggestions or projects, nor had it ever allowed him to deliver his annual report on the state of human rights during his tenure in office.

Prison and Detention Center Conditions

Prison conditions were harsh and life threatening due to gross overcrowding, lack of internal control, and poor sanitary conditions.

Physical Conditions: Prisons and detention centers were overcrowded and underfunded. Pretrial detainees were held with convicted prisoners in all major facilities for as long as five years, according to the NGO Pastoral Penitentiary. On March 9, Director of the Penitentiary System Jorge Lopez Arenas reported the total number of inmates was 13,940. Overcrowding was a serious structural and human rights problem in all major prisons and detention facilities. Palmasola, a prison located in the city of Santa Cruz, was designed to hold 1,800 prisoners but housed more than 5,400 inmates. While the maximum number of prisoners for most cells was four, there were up to 10 individuals in each cell. In the La Paz prison San Pedro, there were more than 2,000 inmates in a facility built to hold 500. The bathrooms were often connected to the living quarters, and the sewage system frequently did not work, causing sewage backups and other unsanitary conditions in living spaces.

Prisoners were largely responsible for paying for their own goods and services in prison because available services to sustain basic needs were inadequate. This included food, lodging, medical care, and transportation to and from court proceedings. Prisoners had access to potable water, but the standard prison diet was insufficient. Since the government's daily allocation for a prisoner's diet was eight bolivianos ($1.17), many prisons depended on donations from other organizations for food. Prisoners who could not afford their own lodging often had to convert bathrooms, hallways, kitchens, and other areas into sleeping quarters. Although the law provides that prisoners have access to medical care, the care was inadequate, and it was difficult for prisoners to obtain permission for outside medical treatment.

Due to persistent corruption, a prisoner's wealth often determined his or her physical security, cell size, visiting privileges, ability to attend court hearings, day-pass eligibility, and place and length of confinement. Inmates alleged there were an insufficient number of police officers to escort inmates to their judicial hearings, and credible NGOs reported that prison directors often refused to help facilitate the transfer of inmates to hearings, further delaying cases. Inmates also claimed police demanded bribes in exchange for allowing them to attend hearings.

Due to a lack of internal policing, violence was ubiquitous and often included systematic intimidation, corruption among prison authorities, psychological mistreatment, extortion, torture, and threats of death. Much of the aggression was prisoner-on-prisoner violence.

There were two women's prisons located in La Paz, one in Trinidad, and one in Cochabamba. In Morros Blancos Prison in Tarija, Montero Prison in Santa Cruz, Riberalta Prison in Beni, and Oruro Prison in Oruro, men and women shared sleeping facilities. In other facilities men and women maintained separate sleeping quarters, but the populations comingled daily. Female inmates were reportedly sexually harassed and/or assaulted on a regular basis, and some were forced to pay antirape extortion fees.

A 2014 law lowered the juvenile detention age from 16 to 14 and requires juvenile offenders be housed in facilities separate from the general prison population in order to facilitate rehabilitation. Any adolescent under 14 years of age is exempt from criminal liability but may be subject to civil liability. The government, however, has yet to build new juvenile facilities, nor have officials allocated the funds required to implement the legal requirements. As a result, hundreds of juveniles between the ages of 14 and 18 were intermingled with adult prisoners in jails due to a lack of sufficient juvenile-specific facilities. Adult inmates and police reportedly abused juvenile prisoners. Rehabilitation programs for juveniles or other prisoners remained scarce.

Although the law permits children up to the age of six to live with an incarcerated parent under "safe and regulated conditions," children as old as 12 resided in detention centers with incarcerated parents, and conditions were regularly unsafe. Despite a 2013 governmental plan to remove children from prisons, government reports indicated that an estimated 3,000 children were living with their incarcerated parents, 1,500 of whom were in prisons and detention centers in La Paz. According to sources, these children had no viable alternative due to economic or family constraints.

Administration: The government initiated a pilot program in the cities of Cochabamba and Cotahuma to digitalize prison records and legal information for all detainees, but it had not been implemented nationwide due to lack of funding. Despite this initiative recordkeeping remained inadequate. Poor records and lack of adequate legal counsel led to cases in which prisoners remained incarcerated beyond the maximum sentence allowed for the crime for which they had been convicted. Prisoners could submit complaints periodically to a commission of district judges for investigation, but, due to fear of retaliation by prison authorities, inmates frequently did not submit complaints of abuses.

Independent Monitoring: The government generally permitted prison visits by independent nongovernmental observers such as the International Committee of the Red Cross, local NGOs, judges, religious authorities, legislative representatives, and media representatives, and such visits took place during the year.

d. Arbitrary Arrest or Detention

Role of the Police and Security Apparatus

The national police, under the Ministry of Government's authority, have primary responsibility for law enforcement and the maintenance of order within the country, but military forces may be called to help in critical situations. Military forces report to the Ministry of Defense. Migration officials report to the Ministry of Government, and police and military share responsibilities for border enforcement. The law to investigate and punish internal police abuse and corruption remained suspended and unenforced as a result of national police strikes in 2012, when the government agreed to revise the code. There was no progress in negotiations between the Ministry of Government and the National Police Association on this problem. Congress did not act on the Constitutional Court's 2012 ruling to adjust the military criminal code and the military code of criminal procedure to stipulate that human rights violations be judged by the ordinary justice system, in compliance with the constitution. Inconsistent application of the laws and a dysfunctional judiciary further exacerbated the impunity of security forces in committing abuses.

Arrest Procedures and Treatment of Detainees

The law requires that police obtain an arrest warrant from a prosecutor and that a judge substantiate the warrant within eight hours of an arrest. Credible reports stated that police did not strictly adhere to these time restrictions, except in cases when the government ordered adherence. The law also mandates that a detainee appear before a judge within 24 hours (except under a declared state of siege, during which a detainee may be held for 48 hours) at which time the judge must determine the appropriateness of continued pretrial detention or release on bail. The judge shall order the detainee's release if the prosecutor fails to show sufficient grounds for arrest. The government allows suspects to select their own lawyers and provides a lawyer from the Public Defender's Office if the suspect requests one. There were 100 public defenders in the country, and approximately 30 percent of pretrial detainees had secured help from the Public Defender's Office. The public defenders were generally overburdened and limited in their ability to provide adequate, timely legal assistance. While bail is permitted, most detainees were placed in pretrial detention or could not afford to post bail. Several legal experts noted that pretrial detention was the rule rather than the exception.

Arbitrary Arrest: The law prohibits arbitrary arrest and detention, but in at least one case security forces seized and held a member of the political opposition, former governor of Pando Leopoldo Fernandez, under legally questionable circumstances.

On February 26, Gabriela Zapata, an employee of the Chinese company CAMC who reportedly had a previous romantic relationship with President Morales, was detained by officials from the Ministry of Government under opaque legal circumstances, according to a reputable NGO. Although the general prosecutor in the case, Ramiro Guerrero Penaranda, eventually confirmed that her arrest followed all proper legal procedures, credible reports indicated that officials apprehended Zapata without an official warrant or court order. Zapata was sent to a high-security prison used to hold convicted felons. She faced multiple charges.

Pretrial Detention: On March 9, Penitentiary Director Lopez warned the prison population could grow by the end of the year despite remedial efforts by the executive branch to reduce the already overcrowded system through granting a series of pardons. Lopez reported in February that 69 percent of all prisoners were in pretrial detention. The law affords judges the authority to order pretrial detention if there is a high probability that a suspect committed a crime, if evidence exists that the accused seeks to obstruct the investigation process, or if a suspect is considered a flight risk. If a suspect is not detained, a judge may order significant restrictions on the suspect's movements.

The law states that no one shall be detained for more than 18 months without formal charges. If after 18 months the prosecutor does not present formal charges and conclude the investigatory phase, the detainee may request release by a judge. The judge must order the detainee's release, but the charges against the detainee are not dropped. By law the investigatory phase and trial phase of a case cannot exceed 36 months combined. The law allows a trial extension if the delays in the process are due to the defense. In these circumstances pretrial detention may exceed the 36-month limit without violating the law.

Despite these rights, denial of justice due to prolonged pretrial detention remained a problem. In March the local Office of the UN High Commissioner for Human Rights reported approximately 78 percent of cases initiated during 2014 continued to the next year without conclusion. These inmates remained imprisoned due to the inability to obtain legal support to complete the paperwork that would free them from prison. Foundation Construir also noted that almost 75 percent of hearings arranged for pretrial detainees were suspended for a myriad of reasons. Complex legal procedures, large numbers of detainees, judicial inefficiency, executive interference, corruption, a shortage of public defenders, and inadequate case-tracking mechanisms all contributed to trial delays that lengthened pretrial detention and kept many suspects detained beyond the legal limits for the completion of a trial or the presentation of formal charges. Many defense attorneys intentionally did not attend hearings in order to delay trial proceedings and ultimately to avoid a final sentencing. The law does not dictate penalties for such actions.

In 2013 Foundation Construir reported prosecutors and judges relied heavily on pretrial detention, thereby contributing to prison overcrowding and judicial backlog. The report found that prosecutors sought pretrial detention for suspects in 77 percent of cases and that judges ordered pretrial detention in 73 percent of cases in which it was requested (54 percent of all cases). In Santa Cruz, which had the country's largest prison population, judges ordered pretrial detention of suspects in 86 percent of all cases.

Felipe Moza, accused of sabotaging a gas pipeline in Villamontes, Tarija, in 2008, remained under house arrest without sentence. In September 2015 his case was suspended for the 114th time in six years. As of December, Moza had been imprisoned or under house arrest for more years than the penalty that he would have incurred had he been convicted for the crime for which he was accused.

Former governor Fernandez, on trial for assault and homicide linked to the death of 11 protesters in Pando Department in 2008, remained under house arrest without sentence. In 2011 his detention period exceeded the three-year limit on detention without a conviction. The Permanent Assembly on Human Rights declared that the judicial system had exceeded all reasonable timelines to determine culpability. Several human rights organizations and activists lobbied the government for his freedom. On July 18, the president of the National Permanent Assembly of Human Rights sent a letter to Morales stating that there was never an "objective investigation to identify the true authors" of the killings in Pando. He further alleged that Fernandez never received due process because of politically motivated accusations and detention by the government. According to the president of the assembly, the government's actions against Fernandez destroyed the presumption of innocence, a constitutionally provided right for all citizens. The citizen collective Bolivian Coordinator in Defense of Human Rights also sent a letter to the president in July requesting Fernandez's release on the grounds of health deterioration. As of December 1, the case had proceeded to final arguments but had not yet concluded.

Denial of justice due to prolonged pretrial detention remained a problem for many citizens. The human rights ombudsman released a document outlining a project that would allow those in jail to receive amnesty or pardons to help reduce the number of persons held in pretrial detention. According to this document, as of June only 31 percent of people nationwide held under pretrial detention eventually received final sentencing. Despite the fact that these prisoners had not been charged or brought to trial, they were held together with convicted criminals. The number of pretrial detainees in prisons throughout the country heavily contributed to the problem of overcrowding. The government's efforts reduced the percentage of individuals under pretrial detention from 84 percent in 2015 to 69 percent during the year. The government's pardon program affected only prisoners who already received their sentences and were convicted of minor crimes and crimes that resulted in less than five years in jail. Many human rights organizations and NGOs were critical of this program, because it did not apply to individuals who were held under pretrial detention. Accordingly, individuals who did not want to risk remaining under detention for years would plead guilty to the crimes they were accused of to receive an official sentence and thus become eligible for the government pardon. As of May a total of 4,953 individuals who may or may not have been guilty of the crimes they were accused of pled guilty in order to be released under this program, potentially violating their rights to due process and a fair trial.

Detainee's Ability to Challenge Lawfulness of Detention before a Court: The constitution recognizes a citizen's ability to challenge their arrest and detention if they believe their life is in danger, they have been illegally persecuted, or improperly deprived of personal liberty. Individuals are allowed to present their case to any judge and request a re-establishment of their rights. The government respected the ability to challenge lawfulness of detention in practice.

e. Denial of a Fair and Public Trial

The law provides for an independent judiciary, but the judiciary was overburdened, vulnerable to undue influence by the executive and legislative branches, and plagued with allegations of corruption. Authorities generally respected court orders but on several occasions levied charges against judges to pressure them to change their verdicts. Judicial experts reported judges and prosecutors practiced self-censorship when issuing rulings to avoid becoming the target of government attacks.

On March 29, the chairman of the La Paz Department Tribunal of Justice, Fernando Ganam, was detained after being caught negotiating a constitutional protection for the telecommunication business COTEL's president, Fabian Guillen. Guillen was accused of corporate fraud. While the legal investigation was in progress, Ganam, three lawyers representing COTEL, a judge, and two prosecutors, among other individuals, were accused of carrying out extrajudicial negotiations to secure a favorable result for the company. As a result of the investigation into this ring of corruption, investigators accused several police officers, and other legal officials of distorting justice in favor of COTEL. As of December 1, trial proceedings for the accused had not commenced.

The head of the Transparency Unit of the La Paz Judicial Council, Ariel Maranon, stated that during the year his office investigated a total of three consortium cases where contingents of judges and lawyers negotiated sentences in an illegal manner. The vice minister of justice and the president of the National Bar Association corroborated this information and added that similar consortiums of judges and lawyers were operating in multiple cities, including La Paz, El Alto, Oruro, Cochabamba, and Santa Cruz. According to these sources, all consortiums operated for "the purpose of extorting and negotiating sentencing and verdicts for litigants."

The judicial budget constituted 0.56 percent of the national budget, which NGOs asserted was insufficient and contributed to an overburdening of public prosecutors and led to serious judicial backlogs. The small budget and inadequate salaries made justice officials vulnerable to bribery and corruption, according to credible sources, including legal experts.

Trial Procedures

The constitution and law provide for the right to be informed of charges promptly and in detail and for a fair, public trial without undue delay. Defendants are entitled to presumption of innocence and trial by jury. They have the right to avoid self-incrimination, consult an attorney of their choice, receive adequate time and facilities to prepare a defense and confront adverse witnesses, present witnesses and evidence, access government-held evidence, and file an appeal. Defendants who cannot afford an attorney have the right to a public defender or private attorney at public expense. There were, however, only 100 public defenders to cover the country. There were 1,004 judges in the country and 850,000 registered criminal cases per year, requiring each judge to handle approximately 850 cases each year. Corruption, influence by other branches of government, insufficient judicial coverage, and a lack of adequate resources devoted to the judiciary undermined these constitutional rights. Free translation and interpretation services are required to be provided to all Bolivian citizens by law. In practice, however, officials complied with this law when there was sufficient budget and personnel.

Political Prisoners and Detainees

There were reports that the government prosecuted several members of political opposition parties for political purposes. The most high-profile case of political persecution and possible detainment for politically motivated reasons was the latest legal investigation of presidential runner-up in 2014 and leader of the main opposition party, Samuel Doria Medina. Congress created a Special Commission of Investigation through which they charged Doria Medina with misappropriating funds, creating damaging contracts, and dereliction of duty during his tenure as Minister of Planning and Coordination from 1991 to 1993. Several government officials, including President Morales, declared Doria Medina guilty of these charges despite the fact that legal proceedings had not yet commenced. The attorney general requested that Doria Medina be detained in pretrial detention for the duration of the legal proceedings. The hearing to determine this detention status was set for November 17. The vice president also accused Doria Medina of tax evasion, and the minister of communications accused him and members of his political party of racism.

The independent news outlet *Pagina Siete* reported on October 24 there were at least 116 legal processes filed against the five most prominent opposition leaders.

Civil Judicial Procedures and Remedies

The law permits individuals and organizations to seek criminal remedies for human rights violations through domestic courts. At the conclusion of a criminal trial, the complainant can initiate a civil trial to seek damages. The human rights ombudsman can issue administrative resolutions on specific human rights cases. The ombudsman's resolutions are nonbinding, and the government is not obligated to accept his or her recommendations.

f. Arbitrary or Unlawful Interference with Privacy, Family, Home, or Correspondence

The law prohibits such actions, but there was at least one case in which the government failed to respect these prohibitions. In 2015 government authorities installed cameras in the home of General Gary Prado Salmon, implicated in the alleged terrorism case against 39 former civic and political leaders of Santa Cruz. Prado, who was in poor health and could not leave his bed, was forced to accept the cameras based on a disputed court order that stated they were necessary to ensure he could continue to testify in his case. Prado challenged the constitutionality of this action, and the Constitutional Tribunal ruled in his favor in July, stating that the government had interfered with his privacy.

There were credible reports that the ruling MAS party required government officials to profess party membership to obtain/retain employment and/or access other government services.

Section 2. Respect for Civil Liberties, Including:

a. Freedom of Speech and Press

While the constitution provides for freedom of speech and press, the government did not allow media outlets to express opinions without some reprisal. Government actions to curb dissenting opinion and criticisms created a climate of hostility towards independent journalists and media. Some media sources reported the government pressured and intimidated them to report favorably about its policies, particularly by withholding of government advertising and imposing steep taxes. Members of the press also alleged government officials publicly harassed individual journalists, both verbally and legally, resulting in several prominent journalists ceasing their work or fleeing the country to avoid legal prosecution. Other sources reported that the government intimidated and threatened media outlets perceived to be critical of the government, in an attempt to censor journalists. Members of the government publicly labeled various independent media outlets and individual journalists as being part of a "Cartel of Lies," in attempts to discredit their reporting; one negative result of such treatment was that journalists practiced self-censorship. Further, the government used its advertising funds to support government-friendly media and deny resources to media it considered critical of the government. The special rapporteur for freedom of expression of the Inter-American Commission on Human Rights noted during his August visit that the government's actions against the media did not contribute to a climate of plurality, tolerance, or respect for freedom of expression.

<u>Freedom of Speech and Expression</u>: On May 10, Minister of the Presidency Juan Ramon Quintana accused Wilson Garcia, the then executive director of the print and digital newspaper *Sol de Pando*, of sedition. During the time of the accusation, Garcia was in the city of Cobija investigating an international human trafficking and prostitution ring that had supposed ties to several government officials. Garcia intimated throughout the investigating his suspicions that Quintana was either directly or tangentially involved in this illegal operation. Shortly thereafter Quintana ordered Garcia to appear in court on sedition charges in the city of Cochabamba. On May 12, Garcia fled to Rio Branco, Brazil, due to fears that he would be arrested if he appeared in court. The judge in the case issued an arrest warrant when Garcia did not appear at his court appointment. The warrant was still active, and legal action against Garcia remained pending.

In May independent journalist Carlos Valverde fled the country after government officials issued threats of legal action against him for publishing articles about government corruption and nepotism. In February, Valverde accused President Morales of involvement in "influence peddling" with Morales' former partner, Gabriela Zapata, and CAMC. In response to this article, several of Valverde's family members reported being followed to and from home and work and harassed by police on several occasions. After Valverde fled, Morales personally commented on this situation through his twitter account, stating, "Whoever hides themselves or escapes is a confessed delinquent, not a politically persecuted person." While the government, including Morales, was absolved of any wrongdoing in the case, Zapata remained in prison under pretrial detention.

President Morales initiated criminal proceedings against well-known journalist Humberto Vacaflor for defamation and slander after Vacaflor publicized accusations that Morales ordered the execution of the Andrade family in 2000. Although other individuals, including a former senator who represented the ruling MAS party, corroborated Vacaflor's assertions, the case against him went forward. On September 28, the judge denied Vacaflor's petition to move the case to an independent press tribunal and gave Vacaflor five days publicly to retract the accusations he made against Morales. On September 29, Vacaflor retracted the accusations, stating the system was too powerful for him to fight. Morales "accepted" the retraction on October 4, and the government apparently dropped the case against the journalist.

During a May 19 address to parliament, Minister of the Presidency Quintana accused the independent newspapers *Erbol*, *El Deber*, and *Pagina Siete* and the news agency Fides of forming a "Cartel of Lies." According to Quintana, this "unit" actively worked in conjunction with a foreign embassy to discredit the government and President Morales. The president, vice president, and other top officials in the government used this branding in an attempt to undermine and silence opposition journalists, columnists, and op-ed writers. Morales also asserted Special Rapporteur for Freedom of Expression Edison Lanza Robatto was aligned with the "Cartel" after Lanza's August 24 commentary on the lack of media freedoms in the country.

In an apparent case of self-censorship, the Red Uno news network fired Enrique Salazar for publicly arguing with Minister of Communication Marianela Paco during a live broadcast on May 20. Red Uno had ties to the government as the wife of Vice President Alvaro Garcia Linera was its main news anchor.

<u>Press and Media Freedoms</u>: Some media outlets alleged the government pressured news organizations to report favorably about government policies and retaliated against news organizations that did not comply. The National Press Association and several journalists alleged the government's retaliatory tactics included withdrawing all of its advertisements, thus denying a significant source of revenue, and launching stringent tax audits, which forced companies to spend time and resources to defend themselves. According to Supreme Decree 181, the government is responsible for providing goods and services to all media outlets in a nondiscriminatory manner. Moreover, the withholding of these government-guaranteed goods and services is in direct violation of Declaration of Principles of the Freedom of Expression Declaration adopted by the Inter-American Commission on Human Rights. There were many credible reports that the government chose not to deliver these goods to media outlets they designated as adversarial to the government. Certain independent outlets did not receive funding from the government after being identified as part of the "Cartel of Lies."

On August 19, Marco Antonio Dipp, leader of the Sucre-based daily newspaper *Correo del Sur*, sent a denunciation letter to the mayor, MAS party member Ivan

Arcienega, claiming that he prohibited *Correo del Sur* from receiving any funds from the municipal government. On August 21, the National Press Association decried the economic asphyxiation of independent media at the national, departmental, and municipal levels. The association also asserted that this financial attack against independent media was made more acute by the February 21 referendum loss, which the government blamed in large part on social media and the press. The secretary general of the municipality stated that Dipp's accusations were false and that the government was not unfairly biased; according to the secretary, it was less expensive for the city to advertise in other publications.

Financial actions on the part of the government appeared to support the claim that the government was trying to control the media narrative. The government increased media investment by 22 percent over the previous 12 months. Further, the Ministry of Communication received a 367 million-boliviano ($54 million) budget allocation for the year, an increase of 260 million bolivianos ($38 million) compared with 2015. Finally, the government invested in the creation of the new General Directorate of Social Networks, an entity dedicated specifically to placing government-friendly messages in social media outlets and engaging in online harassment of social media users who criticize the government on their personal pages.

Authorities disputed the idea that they were economically suffocating any media outlets. Minister of Communication Paco cited the August modification of Telecommunications Law, which provides for broadcasting licenses to broadcast media outlets until November 30, 2019, as proof of the existence of freedom of expression. According to the director of the telecommunications and transportation authority, the modifications of the law would positively affect 135 media outlets. Under the new version, media outlets can retain their licenses until 2019--three years past the original expiration date. Nonetheless, outlets must still bid on their licenses. Critics expressed concern that it would permit government officials to turn bidding into an opaque and unfair process for those media outlets that were critical of the government.

<u>Violence and Harassment</u>: There were reports of violence and harassment against members of the press corps, especially those who reported on the February 21 referendum proceedings and results and on various protests throughout the year. Jesus Alanoca, of the newspaper *El Deber*, and Alvaro Valero were arrested while covering demonstrations in La Paz. The vice minister of the interior claimed that Alanoca was detained because he was not carrying proper credentials to cover the protests, although Alanoca stated that he showed both his journalist credentials and

his government identification at the time of his arrest. Before either was allowed to leave custody, police ordered that they destroy all their footage of the protests. Valero reported being victimized again during the course of his work when he was attacked during a demonstration two days after he was released from police custody. Reporters without Borders noted that the government-affiliated group Satucos intimidated Australian filmmaker Daniel Fallshawn on several occasions for his documentation of the protests by disability activists.

<u>Censorship or Content Restrictions</u>: The government censored journalists, and journalists practiced self-censorship due to fear of losing their jobs, fear of prosecution, and fear of losing access to government sources. According to a 2014 study published by the University of Texas' Knight Center for Journalism in the Americas and the Unite Foundation, 54 percent of journalists reported being censored, and 83 percent stated they knew of colleagues who had been censored. Of those responding, 59 percent admitted to self-censorship. Approximately 28 percent of journalists were censored for topics that could have caused conflict with the government, 26 percent for reasons that could have affected the interests of advertisers, and 26 percent for reasons that could have exposed journalists to lawsuits.

In January writer Diego Ayo published an investigation about the now defunct Indigenous Fund in which he mentioned specific points of corruption in the handling of the fund that caused economic damage to the government. On May 24, government officials who were conducting an investigation into the Indigenous Fund corruption scandal asked Ayo to "correct himself" and remove his work to prevent anyone else from reading the information he published. Additionally, the officials instructed Ayo that the only information about the Indigenous Fund case should emanate from an official government office, thereby prohibiting him from republishing his investigation.

Internet Freedom

The government did not restrict or disrupt access to the internet or censor online content, and there were no credible reports that the government systematically monitored private online communications without appropriate legal authority. Nevertheless, after the loss of the February 21 referendum, government officials proposed two different initiatives aimed at regulating social networks. The government blamed social media attacks against the government as a major reason for Morales' defeat in the referendum. While these measures were not approved, the government managed to pass a supreme decree that establishes the General

Directorate of Social Networks, an entity under the control of the Ministry of Communication, shortly after the referendum loss. This new institution is tasked with directing the government's "dissemination, consultation, and interaction" with cyber communities.

The Ministry of Government publicly warned citizens involved in the August miners' protest against posting any videos on social media of the negotiation process between the miners and now deceased vice minister of interior, Rodolfo Illanes. The ministry stated that any individual found violating this order would face legal consequences. There is no law prohibiting a citizen's ability to publish this content on any social outlet.

In June the Telecommunications and Transportation Authority reported 6.9 million mobile internet users (in an estimated population of 11 million). The connections to the internet from mobile sources represented 96.7 percent of all internet connections. The remaining percentage of individuals maintained the full range of connectivity in their homes. The three main reasons for low penetration were economic barriers, speed deficiencies, and poor access to broadband, which limited access beyond urban areas.

Academic Freedom and Cultural Events

There were no government restrictions on academic freedom or cultural events, although political considerations allegedly influenced academic appointments, and government entities promoted a culture of self-censorship.

b. Freedom of Peaceful Assembly and Association

Although the constitution provides for the freedoms of assembly and association, civil society groups, especially, but not limited to, those critical of the government, faced harassment and threats of expulsion from government officials.

Freedom of Assembly

While the law requires a permit for most demonstrations, the government rarely enforced the provisions, and most protesters demonstrated without obtaining permits. Most demonstrations were peaceful, but occasionally demonstrators carried weapons, including clubs, machetes, firearms, firecrackers, and dynamite. Security forces at times dispersed protest groups carrying weapons or threatening government and private facilities.

Disability activists began protesting during May in the city of Cochabamba to demand an increase in their annual government stipends from 1,000 bolivianos ($146) to 7,000 bolivianos ($1,023). After more than a month of failed attempts to increase the government's financial allocation, more than 500 persons with disabilities traveled to La Paz to demand a meeting with the president and other high government officials. Although they arrived in La Paz without disruption from the police, several citizens verbally and physically attacked the group along the way. The activists also faced public criticism from government officials after the protests began. Health Minister Ariana Campero was one of the most vocal critics of the movement, trying to discredit the claims of the protesters by stating various times that they were carrying out political stunts. She also claimed that the protesters were purposefully attempting to generate the image that the ruling party was insensitive to the needs of this population.

In La Paz on April 27, after a small confrontation between disability protesters and police, the police released what then vice minister of interior Rodolfo Illanes referred to as a "fraction of chemical agent" to ward off the crowd. The action occurred after police formed a human blockade to bar the protesters' entry into Plaza Murillo, where multiple federal government buildings are located. According to sources police released this spray indiscriminately and in a larger quantity than how Illanes described. Video footage provided by the independent news source *Pagina Siete* showed police again attacking protesters who tried to enter the same plaza on May 12. There were also multiple reports of police's using pressurized water tanks against the protesters in an attempt to disperse them.

Freedom of Association

The constitution provides for freedom of association, but the government did not respect this right. NGOs continued to be targets of government officials, including the president, vice president, and government ministers, if they operated in a manner perceived as adversarial to the government. Some NGOs alleged that government registration mechanisms were purposefully stringent in order to deter an active civil society.

On July 4, the Constitutional Court upheld the constitutionality of Law No. 351, which grants legal operating status to NGOs in the country. With the court's ruling, the government may close any NGO working in the country that "does not meet the standards of the law." The ruling came despite the recommendation from

UN Special Rapporteur for Freedom of Association Maina Kiai that the law was too vague and a threat to freedom of association.

In 2015 Vice President Garcia Linera stated the government would expel NGOs that receive international financing and "get involved in politics." Garcia Linera specifically named four NGOs that he claimed were "spreading lies to defend foreign interests": the Center for Bolivian Documentation and Information, the Center of Studies for Labor and Agrarian Development, the Millennium Foundation, and the Earth Foundation. All four had expressed their disapproval of government plans to explore for hydrocarbons in protected areas. Minister of Autonomies Hugo Siles threatened to rescind their legal permission to operate in the country.

c. Freedom of Religion

See the Department of State's *International Religious Freedom Report* at www.state.gov/religiousfreedomreport/.

d. Freedom of Movement, Internally Displaced Persons, Protection of Refugees, and Stateless Persons

The constitution and law provide for freedom of internal movement, foreign travel, emigration, and repatriation, and the government generally respected these rights. The government cooperated with the Office of the UN High Commissioner for Refugees (UNHCR) and other humanitarian organizations in providing protection and assistance to internally displaced persons, refugees, returning refugees, asylum seekers, stateless persons, or other persons of concern.

In-country Movement: The law prohibits travel 24 hours before elections and on census days and restricts foreign and domestic travel for up to three months as a penalty for persons who do not vote.

Exile: In April, Walter Chavez, President Morales' former advisor and former strategist for the ruling MAS party, requested asylum in Argentina due to claims that he was being pursued by the government. Several other former government officials, including Roger Pinto and Mario Cossio, were also in exile.

Protection of Refugees

<u>Access to Asylum</u>: The law provides for the granting of asylum or refugee status, and the government has established a system for providing protection to refugees through the National Commission on Refugees. In September, Vice President Garcia Linera declared the country would not accept Syrian refugees because, in his words, "[t]he situation in Syria was created by the United States and European nations, and they should accept responsibility."

UNHCR reported that 33 individuals from Colombia, Lesotho, Nigeria, and Cameroon sought refugee status in the country as of October. The National Commission on Refugees reached a decision on 31 of the cases, and two additional cases remained pending. Three individuals were granted asylum and 28 individuals were denied. According to media reports, more than 800 refugees from more than 20 countries resided in the country. Most were Peruvian or Colombian and lived in La Paz, Cochabamba, and Santa Cruz. The government did not provide temporary protection or resettlement services to these persons.

<u>Employment</u>: Refugees have the right to work once authorities grant their residency status but not while waiting on pending applications.

Section 3. Freedom to Participate in the Political Process

The constitution and law provide citizens the ability to choose their government in free, fair, and periodic elections held by secret ballot and based on universal and equal suffrage.

Elections and Political Participation

<u>Recent Elections</u>: The government conducted a referendum on February 21 to determine whether or not the president and vice president could run for a fourth term in 2019, thus amending the constitutional provision that bars presidents and vice presidents from serving more than two consecutive terms. In 2013 the Constitutional Court determined that Morales' first term did not count towards those limits because it took place before the passage of the 2009 constitution.

Various events in the period preceding the referendum dominated news cycles and negatively affected citizen's perceptions of the president. One such incident involved the death of six municipal employees from El Alto reportedly due to the actions of a group of protesters affiliated with the ruling MAS party. Government officials accused El Alto Mayor Soledad Chapeton of orchestrating the attack to damage the image of the MAS government. The investigation did not assign culpability to any group.

More than 85 percent of the 6.5 million registered voters voted on the constitutional amendment, with opponents to the amendment narrowly winning, 51.34 percent to 48.66 percent. International and domestic observers reported that voting was mostly peaceful and orderly, with a few exceptions. There were delays in the eastern province of Santa Cruz due to the late arrival of election materials that mandated a revote two weeks after the official referendum vote took place.

The electoral law requires that polls open for a full eight hours on the day of the vote, and observers reported that the government respected the law. The Organization of American States deployed 61 observers throughout the country and generally accepted the voting conditions, even while noting that there was room for improvement on the part of the government. The president publicly announced, two days prior to the official referendum vote, that he would respect the results, regardless of the outcome.

Participation of Women and Minorities: The law mandates gender parity in the candidate selection process at all levels of government. While women had a fair amount of representation on the national level, they remained significantly underrepresented in municipal executive positions. Women participating in politics sometimes faced violence and harassment. In some cases winning female candidates reported threats of violence in order to force their resignation so a male alternative candidate could assume the position. From April to July, the Association of Female Mayors and Councilwomen of Bolivia (ACOBOL) registered 21 complaints of political harassment against women serving in political and public positions as counselors and mayors. According to ACOBOL's main legal adviser, many women were forced to give up their political posts under pressure. ACOBOL also stated that while 21 women made their harassment public, there were many cases in which women feared making their situations public, either for their safety or the safety of their family members.

Section 4. Corruption and Lack of Transparency in Government

The law provides criminal penalties for corruption by officials, but the government did not implement the law effectively, and officials often engaged in corrupt practices with impunity. According to a September poll conducted by the independent news outlet *Pagina Siete*, citizens believed corruption and trafficking of influence were the two principal problems facing the government. The poll found that 44 percent of the persons polled believed the government had serious problems with corruption.

Corruption: There were numerous reports of government corruption during the year. On February 3, journalist Carlos Valverde released a story about his investigation into trafficking of influence between the government and the CAMC. While the government initially denied the charge of influence peddling, the scandal embroiled government officials in the weeks leading up to the February 21 referendum vote on presidential re-election. On February 26, authorities arrested Gabriela Zapata on charges of illegal enrichment, laundering of unjust gains, and influence trafficking, the same charges the government was fighting. During Zapata's tenure at CAMC, the company won more than $500 million in no-bid contracts with the government, allegedly due to her ties to the president. Zapata had frequently worked in the First Lady's office in the Ministry of the Presidency, used a government vehicle, and allegedly had a child with Morales. The formal indictment filed by the prosecution supported these claims, stating that CAMC contracted Zapata because she was "a woman of considerable influence" who had "a direct line to the president of the country."

After her arrest, Zapata accused the ministers of hydrocarbons, mining, and public works, and Minister of the Presidency Quintana of involvement in the corruption scandal. In response, Quintana, Minister of Transparency Lenny Valdivia, and Minister of Defense Reymi Ferreira tried to discredit the claims of Valverde and redirect the conversation by attacking Gabriela Zapata and others in the media.

Although the president was initially reticent on the CAMC affair, mounting political pressure caused him to call for an investigation into the matter of the CAMC contracts. The State Comptroller, an organization supposedly independent but packed with government loyalists, was the first to investigate. The second investigative body to examine the contracts was the Legislative Assembly, where the MAS party holds a supermajority. The Legislative Assembly absolved President Morales, Quintana, and other government officials involved in the contracts with CAMC of any criminal liability. Zapata, along with a lower-ranking official from the ministry of the presidency and a driver of the ministry car used by Zapata, were under criminal investigation and detention as of November. Opposition party Unidad Democrata used the minority report from the Legislative Commission that investigated the matter to allege that the government was guilty of influence peddling in six of the reviewed CAMC contracts. Other civil society and political actors made similar allegations.

In May, Morales' private lawyer filed an additional suit against Zapata and her legal team (Eduardo Leon, William Sanchez, and Pilar Guzman) for trafficking in persons, child abduction, falsifying legal documents, and forgery. Zapata and Morales allegedly had a child together in 2007 that they both claimed died shortly thereafter. According to prosecutors Zapata's lawyers illegally attempted to convince the courts that the child of Zapata and Morales was still alive to show that President Morales had a continuing relationship with Zapata and a reason to support her business ventures.

On July 15, the prosecutor in the case determined there was not enough evidence to sustain any formal complaint against Zapata regarding four of the charges. The prosecutor also absolved the president, the minister of the presidency, directors of CAMC, and other government authorities who were named in the case of any undue influence, corruption, or wrongdoing. Despite these actions, Zapata continued to face a number of charges. On July 27, the government prosecutor presented the following charges against Zapata: laundering of illicit profits, misrepresentation, use of falsified documents, misuse of goods and public services, and conspiracy. As of December she was awaiting trial on these charges in the prison in Miraflores.

Charges against Zapata's lawyers and others embroiled in the Zapata scandal since February were also pending. Police detained Eduardo Leon, one of Zapata's former lawyers, on May 17 after the president filed a complaint alleging Leon was guilty of several crimes, including human trafficking. On June 1, authorities placed Leon in pretrial detention under the charge of falsifying his military record in order to obtain his legal license. Following his initial arrest, the Prosecutor's Office added the charges of fraud and using false documents in official legal proceedings. The Ministry of Education invalidated Leon's legal license because of the accusation that he obtained it under fraudulent circumstances. The National Bar Association stated the ministry did not have the proper legal authority to take such action. Leon remained in custody awaiting further investigation and trial. Two lawyers who were formerly part of Zapata's legal team, William Sanchez and Walter Zuleta, fled the country to avoid facing similar charges by the government.

In 2015 a comptroller audit of the government-run Indigenous Fund revealed that as overseer of the fund, former minister of rural development Nemesia Achacollo, helped divert more than 68.3 million bolivianos ($9.98 million) from the fund. According to media reports, Minister of the Presidency Quintana had known of irregularities in the fund since at least February 2014, and several leaders of social organizations stated that Morales knew of the issue but urged silence to keep unity within the social movements. The attorney general filed charges against Achacollo in December 2015 due to mounting political pressure from citizens. Authorities arrested Achacollo in August and placed her in pretrial detention.

Police corruption remained a significant problem, partially due to low salaries and lack of training. The Ministry of Anticorruption and Transparency and the Prosecutor's Office are responsible for combating corruption, but most corrupt officials operated with impunity.

Cases involving allegations of corruption against the president and vice president require congressional approval before prosecutors may initiate legal proceedings, and congress rarely allowed cases against pro-government public officials to proceed. The government ignored court rulings that found unconstitutional the awarding of immunity for corruption charges.

Financial Disclosure: The law requires public officials to report potential personal and financial conflicts of interest and to declare their income and assets. The law mandates that elected and appointed officials disclose their financial information to the auditor general, but their declarations are not available to the public. According to the law, noncompliance results in internal sanctions, including dismissal. The auditor general must refer cases involving criminal activity to the Attorney General's Office. There were no reports during the year on the financial disclosures of officials or investigations of those disclosures.

Public Access to Information: The constitution provides for the right to access, interpret, analyze, and communicate information freely in an individual or collective manner. No law implements this right.

Section 5. Governmental Attitude Regarding International and Nongovernmental Investigation of Alleged Violations of Human Rights

A number of domestic and international human rights groups operated in the country, investigating and publishing their findings on human rights cases. NGOs and human rights groups working on problems deemed sensitive by the government were subject to verbal attacks and criticism by the president, vice president, and government ministers.

Government Human Rights Bodies: The constitution establishes a human rights ombudsman with a six-year term. Confirmation to the position of ombudsman requires a two-thirds majority vote of approval from both houses of the national assembly, in which the ruling party enjoys a supermajority. The ombudsman is charged with overseeing the defense and promotion of human rights, specifically defending citizens against government abuses. The constitution also affords the ombudsman the right to propose new legislation and recommend modifications to existing laws and government policies. Human rights ombudsmen in each of the country's nine departments report directly to the national ombudsman. The Ombudsman's Office operated with adequate resources. Both houses of congress have human rights committees that propose laws and policies to promote and protect human rights. Congressional deputies and senators sit on the committees for one-year terms.

The MAS party-controlled National Assembly appointed David Alonso Tezanos as the new human rights ombudsman on May 13. Immediately after his swearing-in, Vice President Garcia Linera called for Tezanos to change the institution so that it would no longer resemble the office headed by former human rights ombudsman Villena, who was criticized by the MAS government as being a "demagogue," a "neoliberal," and an "advisor of the right." Upon taking office, Tezanos pledged that the Ombudsman's Office would "cease being a judge of the State" and would no longer issue critical reports. Many criticized the government's choice in Tezanos, stating that the position was designed for individuals free of political affiliations; before becoming the ombudsman, Tezanos worked for the Ministry of Justice and the Office of the Comptroller.

Section 6. Discrimination, Societal Abuses, and Trafficking in Persons

Women

<u>Rape and Domestic Violence</u>: Rape and domestic violence remained serious and underreported problems. The law establishes penalties of imprisonment for 15 to 20 years for the rape of an adult. Domestic abuse resulting in injury is punishable by three to six years' imprisonment, and the penalty for serious physical or psychological harm is a five- to 12-year prison sentence. Despite these legal provisions, conviction rates were low.

On April 11, a young couple was arrested in Cochabamba and taken to the police station. While they were in police custody at the Trafficking and Victims unit, an officer allegedly raped the 16-year-old girl. On April 13, police detained the alleged perpetrator, and the Prosecutor's Office was investigating the case. According to the 2016 UN Human Development Report, eight of every 10 women reported having no confidence in the police in Cochabamba.

The Special Force for the Fight Against Violence (FELCV), a unit within the national police, reported receiving 21,405 cases of domestic abuse, gender-based violence, and rape as of September. Of those cases, 630 were rape cases, and 18,805 cases were of domestic or familial violence. The FELCV's national director, Norma Hurtado, reported 589 acts of sexual abuse in the first semester of the year. Authorities stated that 61 femicides occurred between January and August. The city of Cochabamba registered the largest number of cases (20), with Santa Cruz and La Paz reporting 18 and 16 cases, respectively. Of those killed, 32 percent were raped beforehand, according to police data. Hurtado stated that the principal causes behind these were disagreements between couples, economic factors, and the excessive consumption of alcohol. According to the State Prosecutor, of the 192 cases of femicide since 2015, only 38 percent resulted in the maximum 30-year conviction.

Women's rights organizations reported that police units assigned to the FELCV did not have sufficient resources and that frontline officers lacked proper training about their investigatory responsibilities under the law. Women's organizations also reported the law's stringent penalties discouraged some women from reporting domestic abuse by their spouses, including because of economic dependence. The law calls for the construction of women's shelters in each of the country's nine departments. As of December the municipalities of La Paz and Santa Cruz both had temporary shelters for victims of violence and their children. The La Paz shelter also had coroner's services and a help hotline. The city of El Alto had a women's shelter capable of housing 25 women. While the city of Cochabamba did not own its own shelter, it signed an agreement with Care Center Women to house women in a facility administered by missionaries. A UN Population Fund study released in November 2015 revealed that in rural areas cases of rape and sexual assault frequently did not enter into a formal judicial process for resolution, and courts instead handled them by fining the perpetrator 500 bolivianos ($73) or by subjecting the perpetrator to 20 lashes.

Rape and sexual violence continued to be serious and widespread problems. A 2015 study by the NGO Women's Coordinator found that of the total cases of sexual violence reported through the legal system, 58 percent involved the rape of an adult and 10 percent the rape of a minor. The Center for Sexual Education and Research reported rapists accounted for the second-largest number of 1,700 inmates surveyed, although most rapists never received a sentence and likely remained in pretrial detention. Some cases of sexual violence resulted in deaths. The law criminalizes femicide, the killing of a woman based on her identity as a woman, with 30 years in jail. Activists said that corruption, lack of adequate crime scene investigation, and a dysfunctional judiciary hampered convictions for femicide.

Domestic violence remained a serious problem. A study by Women's Coordinator found that 91 percent of those affected by such violence were women and girls. According to Women's Center for Information and Development, 70 percent of women suffered physical, sexual, or psychological abuse during their lifetime.

Sexual Harassment: The law considers sexual harassment a civil offense. There were no definitive reports on the extent of sexual harassment, but observers generally acknowledged it was widespread.

Reproductive Rights: Couples and individuals have the right to decide the number, spacing, and timing of their children; manage their reproductive health; and have access to the information and means to do so, free from discrimination, coercion, and violence. According to UN estimates, the maternal mortality ratio was 206 per 100,000 live births. Maternal mortality rates were higher among the indigenous population living in rural areas, which were difficult to access and lacked quality health service facilities. The major causes of maternal mortality were linked to obstetrical complications--hemorrhages, infections, complications related to childbirth--and to abortion. According to the UN Children's Fund (UNICEF), the "Juana Azurduy" bonus, a 2009 government incentive that awards mothers 1,820 bolivianos ($266) for attending pre- and postnatal checkups, diminished the infant mortality rate.

Amnesty International reported that barriers to access to sexual and reproductive health services included a lack of information and access to modern contraception. The UN Population Fund estimated that only 41 percent of women ages 15 to 49 used a modern method of contraceptives, and 18 percent of women had an unmet need for family planning.

Discrimination: The law provides for the same legal status and rights for women as for men, but women generally did not enjoy a social status equal to that of men. Traditional prejudices and social conditions remained obstacles to advancement. While the minimum wage law treats men and women equally, women generally earned less than men for equal work. In 2013 the National Statistics Institute reported that the average salary for women was approximately half the average salary for men and that the wage disparity was greater in urban areas than in rural communities. Women reported employers were sometimes reluctant to hire them due to the additional costs, such as expenses related to maternity leave, in a woman's benefits package. The gender gap in hiring appeared widest for positions requiring higher education. Most women in urban areas worked in the informal economy and the services and trade sectors, including domestic service and microbusinesses, while in rural areas the majority of economically active women worked in agriculture. Some young girls left school early to work at home or in the informal economy. The 2012 census showed that the overall literacy gap between men and women fell to 4.9 percent from 12.4 percent in 2001 and was virtually nonexistent among individuals between the ages of 15 and 25.

The rate of female participation in government was high, but there were reports that female policymakers faced discrimination, violence, and harassment.

Children

Birth Registration: Citizenship is derived both through birth within the country's territory (unless the parents have diplomatic status) and from parents. The 2015 civil registry reported that 56 percent of Bolivians were registered within one year of their birth and 97 percent by the age of 12.

Child Abuse: Domestic violence against children and school bullying continued at high rates. The NGO Foundation Paz y Esperanza reported 70 percent of children suffered physical or psychological mistreatment in their homes, schools, or places of work. The ombudsman of children and adolescents reported that 89.5 percent of mistreated children experienced abuse in familial settings. Education Minister Roberto Aguilar estimated 10 percent of children were victims of sexual aggression.

The law proscribes penalties of 20 to 25 years' imprisonment for rape of a child under the age of 14. The penalty for consensual sex with an adolescent 14 to 18 years old is two to six years' imprisonment. The city of La Paz registered 44 cases of sexual abuse of children between January and April. *Sepamos* and *La Foundation Arco Iris*, two organizations that work on sexual violence against children problems, reported that between 2015 and August 2016, there were 159 cases of sexual abuse of children nationwide. According to these same reports, 90 percent of these cases were never legally prosecuted and only 1 percent ended in a sentence for the perpetrator. Of the 159 cases, 73 percent involved abuse by a family member.

Government authorities took action to reduce violence and harassment in public schools, but abuse remained a significant problem. A Ministry of Education resolution mandates that school administrators implement policies to prevent violence and discrimination in public schools. World Vision Bolivia reported 40 percent of children in schools were victims of bullying and 60 percent of students were victims of violence and mistreatment at the hands of teachers.

Early and Forced Marriage: The minimum age for marriage is 14 for girls and 16 for boys. Minors' parents or guardians must approve marriages between adolescents under 18.

Sexual Exploitation of Children: Commercial sexual exploitation of children is punishable with 15- to 20-year prison sentences but remained a serious problem. According to media reports, from January to June 2015, police investigated 229 cases of commercial sexual exploitation of children. The law also prohibits child pornography, punishable with 10- to 15-year sentences.

Displaced Children: UNICEF reported in 2015 that 20,000 to 32,000 minors lived in shelters after their parents abandoned them. According to official statistics, approximately 4,000 of these abandoned children lived on the streets of major cities, 2,000 of them in La Paz.

Institutionalized Children: Child advocacy organizations reported that many government-run shelters housed both child-abuse victims and juvenile delinquents. There were reports of abuse and negligence in some shelters. The La Paz Department Social Work Service confirmed that, of the region's 380 shelters, including centers for abuse victims, orphans, and school students, only 30 had received government accreditation for meeting minimal standards.

International Child Abductions: On January 21, the government signed and ratified the 1980 Hague Convention on the Civil Aspects of International Child Abduction. See the Department of State's *Annual Report on International Parental Abduction* at travel.state.gov/content/childabduction/en/legal/compliance.html.

Anti-Semitism

The Jewish population numbered fewer than 500. Jewish leaders reported the public often conflated Jews with Israelis.

Trafficking in Persons

See the Department of State's *Trafficking in Persons Report* at
www.state.gov/j/tip/rls/tiprpt.

Persons with Disabilities

The law prohibits discrimination against persons with physical, sensory,
intellectual, and mental disabilities in employment, education, air travel and other
transportation, access to health care, the judicial system, or the provision of other
government services. The law requires access for wheelchair users to all public
and private buildings, duty-free import of orthopedic devices, and a 50 percent
reduction in public transportation fares for persons with disabilities. The
constitution and law also require communication outlets and government agencies
to offer services and publications in sign language and Braille. The government
did not effectively enforce these provisions.

A national law to protect the rights of persons with disabilities exists, but it lacked
full implementation and budgetary support. In addition, the law is more than 50
years old, and many of its protections and requirements are outdated. Activists
expressed concerns about the inadequacy of services and opportunities for persons
with disabilities in the areas of employment, education, transportation, health care,
justice, and recreation. They called for greater investment in the area of medical
prevention. In addition societal discrimination kept many persons with disabilities
at home from an early age, limiting their integration into society and restricting
their right to participate in civic affairs. Civil society contacts reported patterns of
abuse in educational and mental health facilities. The National Committee for
Persons with Disabilities, directed by the Ministry of Health, is responsible for
protecting the rights of persons with disabilities.

The law prescribes an annual payment of 1,000 bolivianos ($146) to persons with
disabilities, but activists reported this payment insufficient under cost-of-living
standards. Furthermore, most persons with disabilities were not able to access
these funds. An individual must be deemed "less than 50 percent functional" to be
eligible for the payment and must complete a burdensome and costly
administrative process prohibitive for most applicants. Activists reported a
minority of persons with disabilities benefited from the payment. In May a group
of disability activists initiated protests in the city of Cochabamba to demand a
monthly bonus of 500 bolivianos ($73). The protests continued in the city of La
Paz through October.

National/Racial/Ethnic Minorities

The 2012 census established the existence of 23,300 Afro-Bolivians. Afro-Bolivians in rural areas experienced the same type of problems and discriminations as indigenous persons who lived in these areas. Afro-Bolivian community leaders reported that employment discrimination was common and that public officials, particularly the police, discriminated in the provision of services. Afro-Bolivians also reported the widespread use of discriminatory language. The government made little effort to address such discrimination.

Indigenous People

In the 2012 census, approximately 41 percent of the population over the age of 15 identified themselves as indigenous, primarily from the Quechua and Aymara communities. The government facilitated major advances in the inclusion of indigenous peoples in governmental posts and in society writ large. The government also carried out programs to increase access to potable water and sanitation in rural areas where indigenous persons predominated, although large corruption scandals in the government-run Indigenous Fund inhibited these programs.

Indigenous communities were well represented in government and politics, but they continued to bear a disproportionate share of poverty and unemployment. Government educational and health services remained unavailable to many indigenous groups living in remote areas. On several occasions government-affiliated actors promoted divisions within indigenous organizations to ensure the organizations remained allied with government interests.

Indigenous lands were not fully demarcated, and land reform remained a central political problem. Historically, some indigenous persons shared lands collectively under the "ayllu" system, which did not receive legal recognition during the transition to private property laws. Despite laws mandating reallocation and titling of lands, recognition and demarcation of indigenous lands were not completed.

Acts of Violence, Discrimination, and Other Abuses Based on Sexual Orientation and Gender Identity

The constitution and the law prohibit discrimination based on sexual orientation and gender identity. In May the government enacted Law 807, the Gender Identity

Law, after congress adopted it by a more than two-thirds majority. The law allows members of the transgender community to exercise their right to change their name, sexual identification, and picture on all legal identity cards and birth certificates. Since the law was put into effect on August 1, 50 of the 80 applicants completed the procedure for obtaining new birth certificates reflecting name and sex changes. Further, David Tezanos, the new human rights ombudsman, appointed as one of his deputies the first transgender woman to work in the government. Prominent gay rights activists insisted the government needed to take further actions to guarantee equal family, education, work and health rights for LGBTI persons and also expressed a need for more comprehensive legislation addressing hate crimes and prostitution.

Despite advances, societal discrimination against LGBTI persons was common, even in the highest levels of government. The LGBTI movement was subject to frequent violence and sexual exploitation. In March, three transgender women were killed. LGBTI activists led marches in Santa Cruz on March 25 and April 3 to mobilize the community against such hate crimes.

LGBTI persons faced discrimination in the work place, at school, and when seeking to access government services, especially in the area of health care. The transgender community remained particularly vulnerable to abuse and violence. The Bolivian Coalition of LGBT Collectives reported that 72 percent of transgender individuals abandoned their secondary school studies due to intense discrimination. Transgender activists said a majority of the transgender community was forced to seek employment in the commercial sex sector because of discrimination in the job market and unwillingness on the behalf of employers to accept their credentials. Due to the low wages of most sex workers, the cost of officially changing an individual's identification on government documents (500 bolivianos, or $73) under the new Gender Identity Law is still prohibitive for many in the transgender community.

Elderly LGBTI persons faced high rates of discrimination when attempting to access health-care services, and there were no legal mechanisms in place to transfer power of attorney to a same-sex partner.

HIV and AIDS Social Stigma

The National Coordinator for the HIV/AIDS program under the Ministry of Health reported 16,022 individuals infected with HIV/AIDS. The majority of these cases were concentrated in the city of Santa Cruz, where more than 50 percent of infected individuals lived. The director of the NGO Igualdad reported that approximately 30 percent of transgender individuals in Santa Cruz had HIV. The Ministry of Health registered 32 new cases nationwide of children infected with HIV during the year, and a total of 155 children with HIV/AIDS in the country. On September 14, the La Paz Health Department issued a warning in the Department of La Paz due to an alarming growth rate of HIV cases. From January to August, 347 new cases of HIV infections were reported in La Paz, nine more than during the same period in 2015.

Although the law prohibits discrimination against persons with HIV/AIDS, pervasive discrimination persisted. Ministry of Health authorities reported that discrimination against persons with HIV/AIDS was most severe in indigenous communities, where the government was least successful in diagnosing cases.

The National Network of Persons Living with HIV in Bolivia stated in their 2015 report on the human rights situation for HIV-infected persons that, while social stigmas and discrimination against this population remained prevalent in the country, the situation had worsened for individuals who disclosed their statuses to employers. At least two individuals reported receiving pressure to resign from their positions and reported being victims of other types of discrimination due to their sexual orientation.

In 2012, the most recent year data was available, the Ministry of Health reported 32 percent of the persons with HIV/AIDS surveyed suffered insults or verbal abuse, 20 percent were threatened, and 22 percent were victims of violent aggression. The study also noted that 20 percent of those surveyed reported discrimination in provision of government services at hospitals and schools and that many persons with HIV/AIDS did not report acts of discrimination due to fear. Activists reported discrimination forced HIV-positive persons to seek medical attention outside the country.

Other Societal Violence or Discrimination

Vigilante justice remained a serious and growing problem, especially in rural communities and in El Alto. While no mob violence resulted in deaths during the year, mobs attempted on multiple occasions to hang their victims, set them on fire, or bury them alive.

Mob violence seriously injured several persons during the year. In many cases mobs attacked the victims for alleged crimes, and in some instances police refused to intervene due to lack of capacity and fear of becoming victims themselves. In March a woman welcomed disability activists into her home when they arrived in La Paz (see section 2.b.). Members of the "Campesinos" Federation beat the woman for her actions towards the protesters and threatened to "destroy her land." As of December there had been no official response to the incident.

Most participants in acts of vigilante justice cited the broken nature of the justice system as the principal motivator to pursue justice by other means.

Section 7. Worker Rights

a. Freedom of Association and the Right to Collective Bargaining

The law, including related regulations and statutory instruments, provides for the freedom of association, the right to organize and bargain collectively, and the right to strike. The law prohibits anti-union discrimination and requires reinstatement of workers fired for union activity. The law does not require government approval for strikes and allows peaceful strikers to occupy business or government offices. The constitution provides for protection of general and solidarity strikes, and the right of any working individual to join a union.

Workers may form a union in any private company of 20 or more employees, but the law requires that at least 50 percent of the workforce be in favor. The law requires that trade unions register as legal entities and obtain prior government authorization to establish a union and confirm its elected leadership, permits only one union per enterprise, and allows the government to dissolve unions by administrative fiat. The law also requires that members of union executive boards be Bolivian by birth. The labor code prohibits most public employees from forming unions, but some public sector workers (including teachers, transportation workers, and health-care workers) were legally unionized and actively participated as members of the Bolivian Workers' Center without penalty. The government enforced applicable laws but the enforcement process was often slow due to bureaucratic inefficiency and the lack of funds.

The National Labor Court handles complaints of antiunion discrimination, but rulings took a year or more. The court ruled in favor of discharged workers in some cases and required their reinstatement. Union leaders stated that problems often were resolved or no longer relevant by the time the court ruled. Government remedies and penalties--including fines and threats of prosecutorial action for businesses that violate labor laws--were often ineffective and insufficient to deter violations for this reason.

The lack of financial and human resources for labor courts and the lengthy time to resolve cases and complaints limited freedom of association. Moreover, the 20-worker threshold for forming a union proved an onerous restriction, since an estimated 72 percent of enterprises had fewer than 20 employees. Labor inspectors may attend union meetings and monitor union activities. Collective bargaining and voluntary direct negotiations between employers and workers without government participation was limited. Most collective bargaining agreements were restricted to addressing wages.

Violence during labor demonstrations continued to be a serious problem. In May the National Assembly passed Supreme Decree 275, annulling the president's 2012 executive order outlawing the use of dynamite during public protests. The government overturned the decree in August due to the increased and deadly violence between the miners and police during the August miner's protests.

The government respected freedom of association and the right to collective bargaining. On August 20, President Morales expanded these rights with an amendment that allows for the unionization of subcontractors within the mining cooperatives. The National Federation of Mining Cooperatives reacted with protests and blockades as a result of this amendment, because it directly affected their power. The resulting violent protests left three miners and the vice minister of the interior, Rodolfo Illanes, dead. While the miners claimed police killed the protesters, the government stated that it only used nonlethal weapons and implicated the miners for the killings. The investigation was in progress as of December.

b. Prohibition of Forced or Compulsory Labor

The law prohibits all forms of forced or compulsory labor, yet it remained a serious problem. Labor exploitation, forced labor, and other forms of servitude are punishable with 10 to 15 years' imprisonment for exploitation of adults, and 15 to 20 years' imprisonment for exploitation of children.

There was a lack of enforcement of the law banning forced labor. Ministry of Labor officials noted that the lack of resources prevented more thorough enforcement and restricted the ability of authorities to provide services to victims of forced labor. The Ministry of Labor held various workshops to educate vulnerable workers of their rights, levied penalties and fines against offending employers, and referred cases of suspected forced labor and human smuggling to the Ministry of Justice for prosecution in an attempt to eliminate forced labor. Penalties against employers found violating forced labor laws were insufficient to deter violations, in particular because they were generally not enforced.

Men, women, and children (see section 7.c.) were victims of forced labor in domestic service, mining, ranching, and agriculture as well as sex trafficking. According to the Walk Free Foundation, more than 46,000 persons were victims of forced labor.

Also see the Department of State's *Trafficking in Persons Report* at www.state.gov/j/tip/rls/tiprpt/.

c. Prohibition of Child Labor and Minimum Age for Employment

The 2014 Child and Adolescent Code permits children as young as age 10 to work legally in certain situations, in direct violation of the International Labor Organization's Convention No.138 on minimum age. While the law states that the minimum working age is 14, it also authorizes the Municipal Child and Adolescent Office to permit children as young as age 10 to work if they choose to do so voluntarily, and work independently or with the family. Children must also obtain permission from their parents. Children as young as age 12 can work for outside employers provided they obtain the same permissions. Ministry of Labor inspectors are responsible for identifying situations of forced child labor. When inspectors suspect such situations, they refer the cases to the Departmental Ombudsman for Children and Adolescents for further investigation. The law states that work should not interfere with a child's right to education and should not be dangerous or unhealthy. Dangerous and unhealthy work includes work in sugar cane and Brazil nut harvesting, mining, brick making, hospital cleaning, selling alcoholic beverages, and working after 10 p.m., among other conditions. The Municipal Child and Adolescent Office must answer a request for an underage work permit within 72 hours. The Ministry of Labor is responsible for authorizing work activity for adolescents over 14 years of age who work for a third-party employer. Municipal governments, through their respective Ombudsman for Children and Adolescents offices are responsible for enforcing child labor laws, including laws pertaining to the minimum age and maximum hours for child workers, school completion requirements, and health and safety conditions for children in the workplace. The Ministry of Labor is responsible for identifying such cases through inspections and referring said cases to the departmental Ombudsman's offices.

In June the Ministry of Labor reportedly received funds to conduct a national survey on child labor. By law the survey was to have been conducted within two years of passage of the 2014 Child and Adolescent Code. Ministry of Labor officials confirmed the survey would begin in October or November, with final results released in 2017. The survey was planned for all nine departments.

Labor ministry officials stated that inspectors conducted investigations throughout the year. According to reports, the Directorate General of Labor, Occupational Safety and Health and Fundamental Rights Unit of the Ministry of Labor conducted 43 child labor inspections between January and April. Ministry officials could not give specific inspection numbers and did not have statistics on the number of children they had removed from hazardous situations, although there were specific reports of inspectors referring potential cases of child exploitation to departmental offices of the ombudsman for children and adolescents throughout the country.

Although authorities did not effectively enforce the laws due to a lack of resources, ministry officials stated they had made progress on preventing child labor abuses via the new labor law. According to ministry officials, the 2014 Child and Adolescent code allows officials to have a more accurate count of the number of working underage children. Before the law's implementation, these children would hide from inspectors and observers, distorting the figures. Now that the law protects their employment, they were able to present themselves to inspectors, according to government officials.

The Ministry of Labor dedicated 12 inspectors to investigate child labor and report instances of forced labor and trafficking in persons, two more than the previous year. The ministry, in conjunction with UNICEF, trained these inspectors on child labor and forced labor. The ministry collaborated with the Inter-American Development Bank in April to implement a program that identifies and employs unemployed parents who have children in the work force. A ministry official stated that while there were varying reasons why children as young as 10 chose to work, one main reason was because their parents could not find steady employment. This program employed these individuals under the condition that their children stop working. The ministry also provides the parents' salaries for the first three months in order not to burden the businesses that provide employment.

Despite this progress child labor remained a serious problem. Government officials admitted that instances of child labor violations occurred throughout the country, especially in the mining sector. Officials acknowledged that adolescents ages 15-17 were working in the mining sector unregulated, because it was hard for inspectors to detect these individuals in the mines since they conducted inspections only in the formal sector.

Authorities did not provide information on the penalties for violation of child labor laws or the effectiveness of such penalties, nor did courts prosecute individuals for violations of child labor law during the year, although ministry inspectors referred cases for prosecution.

According to a 2008 International Labor Organization report, the most recent nationwide child labor survey available, 849,000 children, approximately 28 percent of children between the ages of five and 17 worked at least one hour a week. Of the working children, 397,000 worked in urban areas and 452,000 in rural communities. Approximately 491,000 of the working children were between the ages of five and 13, of whom 89 percent worked in dangerous sectors or conditions. Urban children sold goods, shined shoes, and assisted transport operators. Rural children often worked with parents from an early age, generally in agriculture.

Among the worst forms of child labor, children worked in the sugarcane harvest, the Brazil nut harvest, brick production, hospital cleaning, domestic labor, transportation, agriculture, and vending at night. Children were also subjected to commercial sexual exploitation (see section 6, Children). A 2013 study estimated 3,000 to 4,000 children and adolescents worked in the Brazil nut harvest in Beni Department; indigenous groups confirmed a majority of these children were indigenous. Researchers also found that some children worked in Brazil nut processing factories, including at night. Approximately 99 percent of children who worked in the sugarcane harvest in Tarija did not attend school during the harvest, but they may have returned to school upon return to their communities in the remaining months of the year.

There were reports that children were victims of forced labor in mining, agriculture, and as domestic servants. The media reported that minors under age 14 worked in brick manufacturing in El Alto and Oruro, and their parents sometimes contracted them to customers who needed help transporting the bricks.

Also see the Department of Labor's *Findings on the Worst Forms of Child Labor* at www.dol.gov/ilab/reports/child-labor/findings.

d. Discrimination with Respect to Employment and Occupation

Labor laws and regulations prohibit discrimination with respect to employment and occupation on the basis of race, sex, gender, disability, religion, political opinion, national origin or citizenship, language, sexual orientation and/or gender identity, HIV-positive status or other communicable diseases, or social status. Despite these legal protections, discrimination with respect to employment and occupation occurred. Civil society leaders reported credible instances of employment discrimination against indigenous peoples, Afro-Bolivians, and members of the LGBTI community (see section 6). Employers charged with discriminatory practices must offer affected employees restitution to compensate for however the employee was negatively affected.

According to the UN Office on Women, the male population earned between 1.5 to 4 times more than women for the same work. This office also stated that six of every 10 women worked in informal economic sectors and were not protected under any labor laws. In the formal sector, labor laws protect the rights of female employees by providing maternity benefits, breast-feeding hours, and regulations that permit women to work fewer hours than men and entitle women to more holidays in honor of international and local women's days. These laws encouraged companies to hire more men than women, thereby circumventing these regulations, according to labor experts. The former human rights ombudsman for the Santa Cruz Department reported that, in the city of Santa Cruz, a large number of women were fired due to their pregnancies, despite the fact that labor laws protect these individuals while they are pregnant and during the year after they give birth.

e. Acceptable Conditions of Work

The monthly minimum wage was 1,805 bolivianos ($264), an increase of 9 percent from the 2015 national minimum wage. An estimated 45 percent of the population was living below the poverty line, according to credible sources. The government's official estimate of the median poverty income level was 733 bolivianos ($107) per month as of 2013. Labor laws establish a maximum workweek of 48 hours and limit the workday to eight hours for men. The laws also set a 40-hour workweek for women, prohibit women from working at night, mandate rest periods, and require premium pay for work above a standard workweek. The law stipulates a minimum of 15 days of annual leave. The

Ministry of Labor sets occupational health and safety standards and monitors compliance. The law mandates that the standards apply uniformly to all industries and sectors. The government did not effectively enforce these laws.

The Ministry of Labor's Bureau of Occupational Safety has responsibility for the protection of workers' health and safety, but the relevant standards were poorly enforced. The 97 inspectors were inadequate in number to provide effective workplace inspection. The law provides for penalties for noncompliance, but enforcement was not effective, and the fines of 1,000 to 10,000 bolivianos ($146 to $1,460) were insufficient to deter violations. A national tripartite committee of business, labor, and government representatives is responsible for monitoring and improving occupational safety and health standards and enforcement. The Ministry of Labor maintained offices for worker inquiries, complaints, and reports of unfair labor practices and unsafe working conditions, but it was unclear whether the offices were effective in regulating working conditions. According to the law, no worker can be fired for removing themselves from work conditions they deem hazardous. Individuals who are relieved of their jobs can report these practices to the Ministry of Labor and be rehired, if the ministry inspections reveal that their firing was the result of exercising this particular right.

While the government did not keep official statistics, there were reports that workers died due to unsafe conditions, particularly in the mining and construction sectors. Labor experts estimate that "five or six" individuals who work in construction die annually in La Paz. The same sources indicated that most work-related deaths occurred to workers who were employed by small businesses. There were no significant government efforts to improve occupational safety and health conditions. Working conditions in cooperative-operated mines remained poor. Miners worked with no scheduled rest for long periods in dangerous, unhealthy conditions.

According to labor-law experts, the informal sector comprised approximately 65 percent to 75 percent of the economy. These sources claimed that current labor regulations promoted the large informal sector, despite the fact that the laws are meant to protect and promote employee protections. Those working part-time and hourly jobs did not have these protections. Many companies and businesses hired on an hourly or part-time basis.

www.ingramcontent.com/pod-product-compliance
Lightning Source LLC
Chambersburg PA
CBHW080817280726
48660CB00018B/3495